Moxie Moves

10 easy ways to make a powerful difference

Moxie Moves
10 easy ways to make a powerful difference

Sally B. Sedgwick

Cynthia Jane Collins, artist

Spirit Moxie
www.spiritmoxie.com
2019

Moxie Moves
10 easy ways to make a powerful difference

© 2019 by Sally B. Sedgwick
All Rights Reserved

Art © 2019 by Cynthia Jane Collins
All Rights Reserved

ISBN 978-1-7338642-0-6
e-ISBN 978-1-7338642-1-3

Cover design by www.bookcreatives.com

Published by Spirit Moxie
www.spiritmoxie.com

In memory of Jim, who always made a difference to whomever he met and through whatever he did; who always believed in me; and who will always hold part of my heart.

...once or twice [Alice] had peeped into the book her sister was reading, but it had no pictures or conversations in it, "and what is the use of a book," thought Alice, "without pictures and conversation?"

Lewis Carroll*, *Alice's Adventures in Wonderland*

*See Resources, p. 96

Thank You

Giving thanks is a great privilege, or in this case, a gift to actually put into words my appreciation for those who have loved and supported me in this strange process of committing words to paper — and for being the people for whom the words were written.

First and foremost is everyone who either likes the Spirit Moxie Facebook page and/or receives updates from the Spirit Moxie website. Without your encouragement and questions, even in anonymity, there was no reason for this book. The reason became the challenge to make clear in still another way your importance in the world and to me.

But some of you are not anonymous, and I know you well, especially my family and close personal friends. Thank you Pete, Andrew, and Tukta for being slightly amused by your eccentric mom and for your ongoing encouragement. I especially appreciate and love those friends who support the vision of Spirit Moxie: Elizabeth Ring, who read the very first draft of this book and always champions and evaluates; Thea Teich, who struggles to make my prose linear and coherent; Gary Templeton, who uses his multiple skills in multiple ways through photographs, graphics, and web wisdom; Mercurial Puck, who took on the daunting task of editing this text; Linda Kocis, who became a perfect brainstorming partner; David A. Lynch, who supplied proven proofreading skills (although note that any errors are mine, and mine alone); Sandy Eichert and Rick Wiley, who embraced the challenge of making the inside of this book beautiful and easy to read; my original coach Lissa Rankin*, who helped name and form Spirit Moxie's vision; and my current coach Marleen Duval, who constantly offers support and challenge. This book also honors the memory of the creative and talented Michael Philips, who designed the Spirit Moxie logo and created its professional and beautiful brand design.

Plus there are those who have helped me mold ideas, a much more precarious list since it certainly began when I was say, seven, and wrote my first published poem. These are people who, usually unknowingly, have given me encouragement, inspiration, and advice. An endless list, if only because I know I have forgotten many. There are some in "Resources" at the end of the book, but here I give great thanks to Martha Beck*, whose work has instilled in me a conviction that the world works when we follow our true selves, and Shawn Achor*, whose wit and wisdom engages me, and whose statistics give this work credibility with the "fact" that knowing you make a difference makes a major difference in you. Finally, there is J. A. Jance*, whom I wrote to when I referred to her mystery novels in a Spirit Moxie Conversation piece (I was writing about procrastination) and, while she appreciated the reference, took the time to remind me that "real authors write." And so I have.

As I seem incapable of writing at home, my thanks wouldn't be complete without acknowledging the numerous public libraries, coffee shops, and cafés who provide the neutral spaces and reliable WiFi connections that seems to create the only environment where I can consistently even try to do anything creative. So I give special thanks to the Public Library of Cincinnati and Hamilton County, as well as libraries everywhere I travel from Brooklyn to San Francisco to El Paso. (All in the United States.) I don't dare try to begin naming coffee shops, but I am especially grateful to those my computer remembers. It makes working so much easier!

In the midst of writing this book, my friendship with the talented and sensitive Cynthia Jane Collins morphed from a conversation about her doing appropriate black and white illustrations for my ten Moxie Moves into her contemplating and interpreting these ten as multi-media art, showing her own spin and interpretation of these words. Her art expands the vision of this book and, ideally, will do the same with your vision as you contemplate, interpret, and engage with these moves.

If you're not confused enough, somewhere in this process my own identity has changed from "Sally B-," as I've been known since I was ten, to, simply "B," a name that for many reasons feels more centered and fitting. But, yes, I continue to answer to both.

A few of the ten ways to make a difference documented in this book have appeared in slightly different versions as Conversation posts on *spiritmoxie.com*. But here they appear as a set, combined with artwork and suggestions at the end. So this book expands how we dare to make a difference together. *Moxie Moves* will get us started so together we can change the world.

Thank you!

Table of Contents

A Conversation   2

A Letter to You   4

1. Smile   8

2. Be Grateful   16

3. Sleep   24

4. Be Litter Free   32

5. Learn   40

6. Listen   46

7. Love Your Body   54

8. Keep Your Word   62

9. Vote   70

10. Play   76

And now?   82

Exercises and Suggestions   84

*Resources   96

The Artist, and The Art   98

The Author   99

"This, more than anything else, is what I have never understood about your people. You can roll dice, and understand that the whole game may hinge on one turn of a die. You deal out cards, and say that all a man's fortune for the night may turn upon one hand. But a man's whole life, you sniff at, and say, what, this naught of a human, this fisherman, this carpenter, this thief, this cook, why, what can they do in the great wide world? And so you putter and sputter your lives away, like candles burning in a draft."

"Not all men are destined for greatness," I reminded him.

"Are you sure, Fitz? Are you sure? What good is a life lived as if it made no difference at all to the great life of the world? A sadder thing I cannot imagine. Why should not a mother say to herself, if I raise this child aright, if I love and care for her, she shall live a life that brings joy to those about her, and thus I have changed the world? Why should not the farmer that plants a seed say to his neighbor, this seed I plant today will feed someone, and that is how I change the world today?"

"This is philosophy, Fool. I have never had time to study such things."

"No, Fitz, this is life. And no one has time not to think of such things. Each creature in the world should consider this thing, every moment of the heart's beating. Otherwise, what is the point of arising each day?"

> Conversation between Fitz and the Fool in
> Robin Hobb's* *Royal Assassin: the farseer trilogy*
> book II (used by permission)

Dear Fellow Traveler,

I've been struggling to find the right words to express how much you matter. Matter to me for what you already do and can do, but also for what you do for yourself and others. How do I find the right words? How do I share that knowing you matter can make you happier — and more productive — as well as help change the world? What words are there to explain how easy it is for you to make a difference in the world?

Yes, easy. I got really tired of things being hard and then I realized they didn't have to be. On the other side of "hard" was always ease and possibility. What was hard, or at least took awhile, was being able to name that it is true that life can be easy. It involved letting go into angst, pain, and frustration. As soon as I let go, things did become easy. It happened when I finally allowed someone to give me a plan to repay crippling debt. Suddenly the debt was gone. Or at least it seemed that way.

It happened after sitting, keeping watch, as my love and life partner died, taking with him my income, housing, and immediate social network. Somehow through accepting this, the vision of Spirit Moxie was born.

I'd been trying to work on writing something fine and interesting. I had over 100 "if only everyone did this the world would be a better place" phrases. (You know you have some of these.) I figured that if I could add pithy and clever one liners to each, I could write one of those little books you give as hostess gifts. But the pithy and clever eluded me!

Then came the appreciation that only with others does true change and possibility happen. Spirit Moxie was named in California brainstorming with a new mentor. "Spirit" for us all. "Moxie" for the verve needed to pull this off. (For that and as part of the name of a much loved, now defunct, band from Canada). I had put my 100 phrases on index cards and kept the cards and the idea so my mentor and I talked "blogs" (for some reason I don't like that word). Through this conversation the inkling of a vision was born.

Afterwards. I discovered chaos theory and learned a critical mass can morph—positively— into something bigger than we or our actions are individually. In this way the 100+ "if onlys," done by all of us, become the critical mass where positive change is possible. Wow. "The Conversation" (instead of "blog") began on a website and a Facebook page invited people to be part of this.

As I struggled to explain these actions, the idea of Moxie Moves as a way to describe them was birthed through more brainstorming in a Cincinnati bar.

A challenge from others to make the beginning of this book more personal resulted in this letter.

Because the vision of our easily working together to change the world has changed me. As a confirmed generalist, it has given me increased hope and focus. Eased my way through cancer and uncertainty. Allowed me to unexpectedly travel, study with a wide assortment of people, and stabilize my finances. Showed me the importance of hope. As I worked towards a place of simply being (apparently I get ill when I do more that that), the consistent vision that kept me going was always Spirit Moxie's. These are grand words because it is all grand. Larger than I am, but still shareable — again with the help of others. And you. For this is all about you, really.

The whole vision of Spirit Moxie is still focused on small, individual actions. Libraries. I'm writing this in a library. Using libraries helps change the world. I got here on the bus. Appreciating and, yes, using public transportation helps change the world.

So the goal of this little book is that I want you to see that it can be easy, while still being challenging, to make a difference. That making a difference, knowing you matter, adds to your happiness and effectiveness, both personally and in your work.

Ah, but how you ask me? It's best to experience this for yourself. In the pages that follow, I'm giving you a jump start on being more effective, happier, and helping to change the world. My gift to you. Here are ten of my list of over 100 of them with a description, a few challenges, and some exercises to get you started. So do one a week. Or read the whole book and pick one. Or, shoot, embrace two or three or ten at once.

Let me know how it goes!

Love,
B

PS — Be warned this work might be dangerous. I shared these ten words and phrases with my artist friend Cynthia and instead of the simple illustrations I expected, she was prompted into the provocative artistic response that accompanies each word or phrase. These are her interpretations without any reference to my writing. What is your personal take on each one? Would love to share those as well.

1 - Smile

1 - Smile

Of all the things on my "little things that can change the world" list that was the basis for Spirit Moxie, this is the example everyone seems to 1) understand and 2) tell me they already do. I use this as an example when people aren't sure what I'm getting at: "You know those things where you say, 'if only everybody...'?" Blank look. "You know, like smile." Nod of comprehension and then, usually, an "if only everybody..." of their own.

The other side of "smile" is the response, "I already do that." Well, so do I, but do we really? I know that I really don't smile all that much. So for me, if I'm honest, this is a real challenge. I've even had awesome encounters where street people have called me out on this. "Why do you look mad? Smile!" (Yes, yes, I was in my head about something.)

So watch yourself. Catch yourself if you are so engrossed with your thoughts that you aren't smiling. I realize many of us don't walk down the street very often anymore, but, when you do, are you smiling at people? Who smiles at you?

"Oh, people don't look at each other, much less smile, in my city." Really? So be weird about it for awhile. Look for an opportunity to catch their eye and smile. Try it in grocery stores. To that rich looking dude in the suit. To the person who might be after a buck. (It doesn't mean you have to give them anything. Just that you admit they're human.)

I remember the time I got out of my car in the grocery store parking lot and the kid wrangling shopping carts flashed me a smile. Suddenly I felt feminine, attractive, interesting, and even a bit sexy. Didn't know I was missing these feelings, but that smile was, really, that powerful. Don't know where it came from. I could invent all kinds of explanations on what it was really about. But it doesn't matter. I still remember it. It still changed my mind and my day.

There is research, and lots of writing, that says smiling is good for you. Andrew Newberg* in his book *How God Changes Your Brain* has "Smile" as number eight in his list "8 Ways to Exercise Your Brain." I think it is only number eight because it is the most obvious, but apparently smiling actually makes neurological changes. There is evidence that smiling helps you stay healthy and increases your sense of well being.

Smiling seems to be popular with researchers and bloggers, bosses and babies. One example is an article by Naomi Simson, Founder of RedBalloon, who talks about always carrying one with her and making smiles genuine. This is the basis of getting this right.

But that's the rub isn't it? Is it right? There seem to be all kinds of ways to smile. Is it a genuine smile? Do they really mean it? What's with that tight lipped look? Yeah, I'll never trust anyone who looks like that... Oh, no. What if I look like that when I smile? (I'm still looking for someone to coach me on what to do with my expression when someone takes my picture.)

Or even, "Why should I smile at that idiot? She just thinks she's better than I am." I'm not making this last one up. Apparently people who feel powerful, even unconsciously, don't smile at people who they think might be better than they are. Smiling apparently gives the other person power you don't want them to have. Confused yet? But I wouldn't take this research too seriously. If you want to expand your life, be healthier, and help change the world —yours and others—keep reading!

Remember that the point isn't what others do. This is about the small things you do. Challenge the perceptions of why you smile and how you read others' smiles. If you must, just smile to help yourself. Apparently when doing yoga a small, half smile helps you have a better workout. It sends messages to the brain that you can relax and all is well - and it has nothing to do with if you mean it. In fact turning up the corners of your mouth regularly can change your day and your perspective. (A famous physiological study showed that if you hold a pen in your mouth so you're "smiling" it increases endorphins too. True.)

Practice smiling at people as you walk down the street or cruise the grocery store, not because you're happy, but just to elicit a response. It's about wishing them a good day, great life whether they see you or not, not about how you are. It's also a kind of experiment in case you just like messing with the universe. Can you make them smile even when they look down? When they're on their phone? When... However you are feeling, I'm betting that after the third interaction your mood will be up and you find yourself looking for the most unlikely person to engage. That toddler who is "playing" with you when his mom isn't looking? The well coiffed woman at the corner who will barely look at you? The homeless dude who values an acknowledgement he's human? (My personal rule means I seldom carry money and don't give it out on the street. But a smile and a shrug to the genuinely homeless almost always elicits a "God bless," a smile, and/or a "have a great day.") And then there's the TSA agent when you leave your driver's license at security. (Yes, well, a rueful smile was all that was needed there.) My favorite is getting the checkout person who is having a no good, terrible, very bad day to smile at least a little. And yes, notice when you don't smile (I'm important and so I won't smile at you? I'm so tired and not sure if that person will engage? I'm scared?) and try one anyway.

This morning I walked around the block, mentally wishing everyone well. Most people deliberately didn't look at me or anyone else, but I shared a "how are you?" "good morning" and, of course, a smile, with a street worker. The door guys at the fancy hotel brightly smiled (usually they're too busy talking to each other). Though I thought the woman engrossed with her cell phone wouldn't look up, she did and we exchanged smiles. And I sent others on their way through a smile whether they saw it or not.

As Mother Theresa said, "Let us always meet each other with a smile, for the smile is the beginning of love."

Okay. Think of the different times people have engaged you with a smile. Remember holding that baby. Or how an appreciative smile adds to a complement. That's right!

Smile as you read this. Yes, as you begin each of the other nine Moxie Moves greet it with a smile. ✻

2 - Be Grateful

There's a trend on the Internet, maybe particularly on Facebook, to post a daily gratitude such as that a friend came to visit or a new office had opened. One year on Thanksgiving Day, Spirit Moxie asked people to list three things for which they were grateful. The responses included the love of a good woman, wonderful and patient friends, family, technology, and "the magical effects of yeast and grapes." What's interesting about this is that it has been shown that gratitude, giving thanks, can actually hard wire the brain to be more positive and more productive. Thanks makes our minds work more easily. And maybe that helps us smile as well.

Why might this be true and what difference does it make? If you "become positive in the present" rather than feel happy only as a response to some event, such as a raise or a compliment, you are actually more productive and successful. In other words, it's been proven that happiness leads to success rather than vice versa. And I'm guessing that most of you reading this would like success in some form or other. When you are positive in the present, you are not dependent on events for your happiness. According to Shawn Achor*, author of *The Happiness Advantage*, you can rewire your brain through 21 days of two-minute exercises: a) think of three new things you're grateful for; b) journal for two minutes about something you're grateful for; c) exercise; d) meditate; e) send a random positive email to someone. You don't need to do all of these activities. From what I read, you just do one a day and you can stick with that one or, the next day, do a different one.

Happiness first leads to a more effective life for us and, as a result, leads to a better life for those around us.

I have a friend who tells me he tried this and it didn't work. So he's figured it doesn't matter. He decided even that, maybe, being grateful makes things worse. So he will tell me over and over again that terrible things always happen to him. Usually he's just received notice of an unexpected repair on his house or car or has been stood up regarding a job opportunity. Or, something electronic didn't work as quickly as he'd like. But on that same day I happen to know he had had a drink with friends, gotten another call about a job he'd rather be doing, and had a real encounter with that cute redhead. Shoot, he may have gotten a check, a professional compliment, and found a new band he loves. But those don't matter. That it all sucks is the only reality here. And no words of mine will change that. If I offer any, he can't hear them.

My friend isn't the only pessimistic person out there. Perhaps you, too, have survived by being negative and looking on the dark side. It's a kind of protection and perhaps even a chosen identity. No surprises that way. But is it really working? Is your life and world what you'd like it to be? If you've really given up, I don't think you would have read this far.

So the question becomes (for all of us) whether being grateful changes you. Or more observably, can it change your world? Science and general experience says it can. And when your world changes the world as a whole does as well, if only by definition. So for, let's say a week, although I'd rather we played with a month, practice gratitude. How? Well, begin here. What is one, small, tiny, very specific thing you are grateful for right now? Claim something that is part of this particular second. Maybe you just like the word "specific." Perhaps you're at least amused at finding this book and you like being amused. Did the dog just push against your leg or the cat get in the way of reading? Is there red in the rug and you like red? I'd love to hear how tiny a thanks can go.

Now pick a big focus for gratitude. It could be something around family, work, or health. It could be exciting news.

Next choose an average focus. Something you just notice and are grateful for. These nourish us and with practice you'll find yourself noticing them all the time.

I'm a stickler for saying that my gratitude and way of doing things isn't yours, so I'm leery of giving examples. I'll play if you promise you'll come up with other things. A tiny thing is that my hair feels soft on the back of my neck. A huge thing is the support I'm getting around possibly moving and so sorting possibilities for my future. And in-between? Seeing a friend. Finding a dollar. The way the sun shines on the leaves of the trees after that fabulous thunder storm (with needed rain). Oh, wait - maybe that last one was two "in-betweens." You don't need to categorize them, but list five a day. If you find yourself repeating the same things, write them down and make yourself change them, narrow them if you will. The more specific you are the better.

  I go through the previous day and find at least five things to be grateful for from that day before I get out of bed in the morning. My list today: Finding the right word. Seeing a lizard dart under the deck. Finding everything I needed on sale at the grocery store. Promptly getting a return email confirming I'll see friends this evening. Seeing some response to a social media request.

  On another level, noticing things to be grateful for helps you not miss what is going on around you. Perhaps that unexpected email, that was a tad humorous, is actually a business lead. Finding the bananas you bought yesterday still in your bag reminded you to brush your teeth before you walked out the front door (OK, maybe not for you. But this happened this morning.)

Breathing. I'm grateful that I can automatically breathe. OK, need to make that more specific. That I can now get my stomach to expand when taking in a meditative breath. What fun it is to have a breathe app on my watch. That I wasn't so out of breath going up the stairs. That it is easy to breathe through my nose. The smell of honeysuckle when I walked around the block...

It can get overwhelming in a good way. Feeling so full of thanks that truly only goodness can creep in around the edges. Take one little bit and keep going. A hundred ways to look at friendship. Two hundred words you love. Three hundred.....

Oh, and thank you! ✿

3 - Sleep

So we understand smiling. And, if I insist, being grateful has been proven effective. But sleep? There's something insidious about the idea that you might be able to change the world by taking a nap. Or by getting a solid 7-9 hours every night. But it's true. It affects how you are able to show up for the world. You don't believe me?

First of all, lack of sleep has been cited as one of the major health risks in the United States. It contributes to type 2 diabetes, heart disease, poor eyesight, weight gain, and sexual disfunction. It also lowers the immune system so you're more apt to go to the doctor for everything from colds to cancer. Lack of sleep is also a cause of major motor accidents, a source of poor judgement, and contributes to depression and ADHD behavior.

Enough sleep improves creativity, athletic performance, and the ability to learn. Plus it increases longevity and makes your skin look better.

May I stop writing now? I don't even need to cite my sources. A click on any Google search result lists pretty much the same attibributes for either sleep deprivation or sleep benefits. There seems to be a little discrepancy on the amount needed. Six to nine hours seem to be the magic numbers, with seven and a half to eight being optimal. (There is some inconsistency in this number, although adolescents and children definitely need more.) And yes, maybe your Uncle Ted did fine on three hours a day, but that is a small minority.

And then there is the question of naps. I'm lucky in that often ten minutes will completely refocus me and this can be a respite from emotional tension as well as physical weariness. One study suggested that men need naps more than women, but the very best advice I've heard is that if one is tired — or maybe just confused, irritable, or stuck — sleeping is one of the best solutions there is. When you can't focus or think clearly, it very often means you need to lie down for awhile. If you think you're sleeping to avoid things, perhaps it just means you need to catch up from years or decades of being on other people's schedules.

Recently I was seated next to a nursing student while on a train trip. "I'll probably fall asleep so just wake me up if you need to use the toilet."

"Oh, I'll just step over you. But interestingly. I'm writing about sleep."

"I can tell when I've been up too long. I get loud and impatient."

"Well, take a nap. Naps are good."

"Yes they are!"

In the end I think I slept more than she did, but the point was made. And apparently she was headed for a break and would "catch up" over the weekend.

Which raises another point. Can we, do we, catch

up on sleep? While it's a brilliant theory. "I'll sleep this weekend," in point of fact that seems to be statistically and physically impossible on an ongoing basis or as a "cure" from extreme sleep deprivation. Those who, for whatever reason (often just to see if they can), go without sleep for days report suspected side effects years later. (Yes, this has also been used in torture. Enough said.) If you plan to try it, please warn me so I can be somewhere else. The affects are not pretty.

But how much does this matter and how do we know? Studies have shown that people who don't get enough sleep become less efficient both physically and mentally — but think they are as efficient as ever. Deep sleep (also called slow wave sleep) is when the body repairs itself. Note that it is harder to wake up when one is in deep sleep. REM (rapid eye movement) sleep renews the brain and helps it process things (which may be why solutions to problems seem to become evident overnight or maybe during that nap). Both of these keep the body whole. As James Clear, the creator of the Habits Academy, says, "Without the slow wave sleep and REM sleep phases, the body literally starts to die."

I have a friend who claims ADHD and always tells me that she didn't sleep — or if she did sleep how her body isn't used to it and she feels terrible. A no win scenario. I can't "fix" her either.

At this point I want to be clear that I'm not claiming any expertise on curing sleeplessness or any other sleep disorder. There are fabulous coaches who have that expertise and all the benefits of sleep are fairly common knowledge. Because I really do care that you, and my friend, get enough sleep let me make some suggestions, as if you were super desperate and we were sitting over a cup of herbal tea. Here are some things to try and you can let me know how they work. First just suppose she (and you?) really worked on being in bed the right number of hours rather than worrying about whether she actually slept. My suggestion for this (and yes, it doesn't always work) is **1)** thank your mind for sharing about worrying about sleep and start giving thanks for other things as well. **2)** Relax into your body — how does it feel touching the sheets? Hmmm, feels good to stretch that knee a little, think I'll worry about that little bit of scratch on the back of my throat tomorrow. **3)** Let your mind go where it will, if you're solving a major problem let it go there but don't engage much. Thank it for working on it. Start playing with absurd answers. **4)** "Daydream" a little. **5)** Relax. Put your mind in wandering mode. I promise you are sleeping more than you think you are. ("I didn't sleep at all." "Well you sure sounded like you were." or, true hospital story of one night when I'd have sworn I didn't sleep, "When I came in to check on you, you were sound asleep.") But keep practicing. AND DON'T WORRY ABOUT IT.

Because another benefit of sleep worth relaxing for is that it can change our relationship to time. Yes, time. When you are rested and working on a project you often can get two or three days worth of work done in half the time. Heck, I've done what I thought was two or three days worth of work in a few hours.

Try it. Rest. Don't watch the clock or give yourself a deadline. Start – *and see what happens.* ✻

4 - Be Litter Free

Originally this section was called "Don't Litter." But all the other Moxie Moves were positive. So we tried other ones. "Respect"? "Dispose of Properly"? But somehow, for our purposes here, the only word that fits is "litter." Somehow litter has become symptomatic of our relationship with things and, by extension, one another and even ourselves.

For years I craved the super power that, when I saw someone throwing something on the ground or out a car window, I could make that same something rise up and glue itself to the person's hand — or maybe just go back in their pocket or back through their car window..

On a more realistic note, for me, whoever is littering just seems tremendously selfish and untrustworthy. For me a litterer is someone who doesn't care about others or their surroundings. So not littering is one way for staying in my good graces, as well as a way to keep the world beautiful.

Not littering was instilled in my children and I'm usually looking for trash cans or finding odd pieces of paper in my pockets. However it is a lot more important than that. Litter both reflects what is perceived about the world around us and contributes to problems in the environment.

Let's begin by considering our perceptions. First litter looks terrible. While this is a subjective statement,

I have yet to find someone who appreciates a McDonald's wrapper on their lawn, a cigarette butt in a lake, or a pile of trash thrown into the woods. Most people associate clean streets with good neighborhoods and higher property values. Cleaning up an area, and keeping it that way, is an automatic, and free, sign of neighborhood improvement. On the other hand if one is evaluating neighborhoods, litter automatically lowers that neighborhood's value. A study in the UK showed that litter lowers the value of a home by up to 12%. And at least 2%.

Litter also affects how safety and crime interact. While I can't find actual statistics, there seems to be general agreement through any online research that increased littering is related to increased crime. When trash is around it is said that it seems to give permission to break other societal rules. So seeing litter, or even more tellingly seeing people litter, increases the likelihood of it being OK to do things like destroy property (even "little" things like destroying signs or adding graffiti), rob, or steal. Litter even invites people to engage in more violent crimes. And I'm not just talking about things like shootings. Most places that have been pointed out to me as major places for drug deals seem to be slightly ill kept, and have a least some litter. So not littering is actually improving, by extension, your personal value as well.

To be fair, often there seems to be no appropriate places in public to put litter. For example, while I may decry smoking, finding hundreds of cigarette butts near a potentially beautiful bus stop with no trash can probably said more about the city than the passengers.

Another example and part of the general hearsay statistics I've lived with for a long time says that crime in the New York City subway system, and even on New York streets, went down as the streets became cleaner and litter got under control. (Note that, those responsible for that bus stop!) And even without statistics, various experiments have shown that decreased littering decreases crime.

The second major category is how litter affects the environment. Litter threatens our wild life by contributing to the pollution that affects water quality (so it affects us too) and often hurts air and soil. It also physically affects wildlife. For example the plastic rings connecting six-packs get around the heads of fish and otherwise tangle in ways that can't be undone. And what is an oil spill except an example of extreme littering? Are you sure the emissions on your car or truck meets the right standards? Did you pour chemicals such as motor oil on the earth rather than disposing of them properly? These are examples of ways to not litter that could indeed save the world as we know it.

In my family not littering outside is a way of life. I still find odd pieces of paper in my pocket. But somehow it gets more complicated inside. Personally it is a war I have with papers - and the papers usually win. Most recently it was a cat strewing business cards over the floor (along with anything else she could find) while staying at a friend's where my things don't have logical homes. With my kids it has been papers and food containers in cars, and clothes and books on the floor of their room, or dirty dishes and stuff on the kitchen counter. An instant party prep was putting everything into neat piles and cleaning the kitchen. This kind of litter affects health (quite literally in the kitchen example) and a sense of order and well being. (For the record, when living by myself, with places for things and a dishwasher, you could come over any time!)

How do you present yourself and your belongings? A messy desk probably cost me a job when working with my paper-free-desk boss. Or ask any professional driver like a taxi or Uber driver. How clean your car is is what gives people confidence and makes you look professional. I still remember a messy car trunk when an Uber driver picked me up for the airport. I'm pretty sure I didn't even bother to rate him much less tip him.

It has been said that a weed is any plant growing where you don't want it, where it doesn't belong. A rose in a corn field is a weed. Think of "things" the same way. That piece of paper is litter on the street, but not in a trash bin or a briefcase. That sock on the floor has a home on a foot, in a drawer, or in the laundry.

Finally we can see how the thoughts, and maybe things, we inflict on others and ourselves litter our minds and our bodies, and by extension the minds, and perhaps physical well being, of those we encounter. This is an insidious idea and is reflected in other ways in other "little things that can change the world" such as "Listen" and "Keep Your Word." But play with this image awhile. How are you littering the well being of you, your friends, and family?

What is your personal challenge regarding litter? As I walk or ride, I see people litter and people picking up litter. I hear and see people disregarding their actions and their words. What can you change about the way you arrange and dispose of things? About how you treat others and how you treat things? About the way you treat yourself? Are you getting rid of the weeds? Who are you for the world? ✲

5 - Learn

Rested? Smiling? Thankful? When I first wrote my list of ten Moxie Moves for this book, remember, I have notecards with over 100, "Learn Something New" seemed an obvious one to include. And then I realized it was a bit redundant. You don't learn something you already know. By definition it's new! But "learn" definitely belongs here. Learning is something that keeps one alert, alive, and interesting. Certainly this is a crucial piece of changing the world. However unlike the other nine, there's no Internet (in this case, aka Google) agreement on learning's powers. There are lists of why it is important to keep learning and personal stories on how "lifelong learning" expanded and changed the writer, but there isn't any agreement on what "Learn Something New" means, and "Learn" is just defined.

What is "learn" as a mandate? Does learning include just doing something differently or in a new way? Is it trying a new recipe or eating something one has never tried before? Taking a different route to work? Trying to write with your non-dominant hand? Or does it only count as learning if you take on some major challenge? Does it only count if you're suddenly learning Chinese or taking up the hammered dulcimer? Through this book we're learning to claim daily actions to change the world and ourselves. That counts, right?

And when does what you are learning become the

norm? That is, when is it no longer new, and the challenge becomes time to learn something all over again? Is my new obsession with stock options fine or, since I've been working on them for several months, does it mean I "should" also start taking ballroom dancing? Is "new" discovering a new author in your favorite genre or exploring a new genre altogether? I assume my embracing a friend's obsession with Formula One racing counts?

The simple answer is yes. Whether a new recipe or a new language, changing a pattern or engaging in deep study, learning in any form expands who you are and what you do. If you try a different route home, deliberately smile at more people, or become determined to — or even just play a bit with— writing with your non-dominant hand (i.e., writing left handed for those naturally right handed or right handed for those naturally left), your brain finds new pathways. That is you continue to "rewire" your brain. (I realize that's not the most scientific explanation. Perhaps exploring brain patterns is something else to learn!)

And the accepted reasons to learn are simple too. Learning keeps us alert and younger. It helps us be a more interesting conversationalist ("Hey, I'm learning to play bridge!" or "I was just reading about that."). Learning can actually be fun and engaging.

But on a bigger scale, learning also makes it

easier to admit we're wrong. Being willing to be wrong is another, and perhaps bigger, leap on the little things we can do to make the world a better place list. It is one that even more obviously can change the world. How so? Let's pretend you are convinced the world is flat. It looks flat! And then you see (and know they are real) pictures of the earth from space. Admittedly, you have an edge here over Pythagoras, or even Columbus, but through seeing the pictures you're willing to give up your "the earth is flat" belief. And you can start playing with the implications of a round world. (And, no, you can't dig a hole to China to see if they're upside down.) Understanding more accurately how the physical world we live in "works" allows us to put everything from politics to the environment to travel in a more accurate perspective. And that doesn't even consider the thought you might, yes really, you, might be wrong in a certain situation, have misread the "facts," or just gotten angry for no real reason. Learning might simply involve seeing any of the above as new perspectives.

     You can see that new thoughts and new ideas, whether the thought is finally understanding what your mother-in-law is dealing with or why those flowers in your garden are dying (it was slugs) or how to pay more attention at work, help us deal with things in new ways. It is from this place that a lot of creativity happens. And creativity is certainly a place of world change, if only by creating new paths and possibilities.

How are you continuing to learn? I joke about learning to run a sound board in another lifetime. But maybe that lifetime is right now. What about you? Dreams? Ideas? Challenges? ✾

6 - Listen

Now that we're excited about what we're learning, we come to the flip side of interacting with others: listening. When asked, a lot of people list "listening" as one of their gifts. While admittedly, this is just something I've observed, I don't think any of us are as good at this as we say we are. I don't think the word is really "listening." The point is do we "hear" one another? *Do we actually get what people are saying?*

There are multiple parts of helping to change the world connected with this. I would like to suggest that this is one of the most life changing parts of practicing being present. For "practice" is the right word. Unless you are, maybe, Eckhart Tolle* at his best, you miss really being with the things around you all the time. And unless you're a hermit (although historically they had to interact with people too), people talk to you. So just to be practical, it is good to hear what is said to us. Answer, respond, and admit if something is unclear. "Why, yes, I'd love the salad." "Hmmm." "We're boarding now? I didn't hear if my zone was called."

It is also how we learn. You know when you look at the notes of the person sitting next to you because you missed that last point during a lecture? Perhaps because you were writing? (The brain is not designed for multi-tasking, no matter what you believe.) More likely you missed that point because you got distracted (did I really turn off the oven? did he say we should or shouldn't do that?) and stopped hearing.

Even more importantly, things change when we can truly figure out what people we think we disagree with are saying. We might still disagree. We may have a brilliant alternative to their problem. But when we can repeat what they mean rather than share our own wonderful truth, they are more apt to hear our response.

When you truly listen, you often can hear what is underneath the words. Hearing rather than listening allows us to at least try to more deeply understand the person we're listening to. They are bragging, but you can hear their fear. They are boasting and you can hear their loneliness. They are putting themselves down, but you know they are proud of what they've done. It is from this place that you can respond to what is really going on. First to check out if what we think we hear is true. This one is tricky. Don't assume what you think you heard is there. Rephrase it a bit: "Is it ever a little threatening to deal with that problem?" "I'm glad to hear you share that." "I don't know—I think responding that way was brave." "You're OK." "We love you." "What you've accomplished is truly awesome!"

So how do we listen? There are a couple places to begin.

First, do you want to? Just because some noises are coming out of someone's mouth doesn't necessarily mean you have to pay attention. Make a polite excuse and walk away. If you're stuck (and not hearing won't come back to cause you trouble), practice really noticing other things. How the colors around you interplay. What the background noises are doing and what they might mean. How your body feels. What does the air feel like on your skin? In other words, this is an opportunity to be present. It just doesn't demand concentrating on that particular stream of words.

Let's say you have to have at least an idea of what is being said. You might be asked to respond or to take some action. If you're genuinely not interested, use it as an exercise. Can you understand the words clearly? Can you follow their train of thought? Could you repeat the general idea, or even their exact words? What is their tone saying? Did they speed up or slow down? What might be behind that? You see, the trick is to focus on them, on their words, almost as things. Since they have nothing to do with you.

Then there are the times when you want to hear. It's something to learn, maybe instructions or a class lecture. Maybe there will be a test or it's just something in which you have a genuine interest. Perhaps it's your partner or lover talking and you truly want things to be right. You are pretty sure those words do have something to do with you. Can you repeat the words? And again, try to figure out how you would rephrase the words to make certain you have the correct sense of them. If you think you need to take notes, remember you will probably miss some things. If that doesn't really matter (because that one point was so brilliant), go for it! If it's being recorded, you might want to wait to take notes later. If you're tired, drink some water — or try yawning which is one of the bodies ways to become more alert (really). Plus yawning is good for the brain. Talk to someone about what you've heard as soon as possible.

Finally, there is conversation. Those times when you really are engaged with someone else. First, if you're not listening, admit it. "Sorry, darling, I was looking at the computer and didn't hear what you said." "Did you see that last shot? Now, what were you saying?" "Day dreaming. Could you repeat that?"

Second, if you genuinely don't understand what someone is saying because of either their accent or tone or your hearing ability, or even because you're so tired you can't think straight, admit that too. Even if the person talking gets frustrated, they would rather repeat (and repeat) if they want to be heard.

Most crucially, don't figure out your brilliant response. One of the main reasons we don't hear someone is because we're impatiently waiting for our chance to speak. Personally, I have a habit of interrupting, because (or so I say) when I first encountered large families (I'm an only child) I learned that was the only way to get a word in. But unless the interruption is important ("dinner is ready"), no one cares. So we say we spend our time "listening," but we are really figuring out what we are going to say. Why what the other person is saying is wrong, or how it could be improved.

Stop! Now! Hear them. Perhaps you've met a potential new friend and you want to hear what they are about. Your response will still be there when they've made their point. If they are one of those people who talk forever and you have to say something, make it brief. You could repeat what they just said.

For a crucial part of listening is understanding what someone is saying. When I told a friend I didn't want french fries with a sandwich, he assumed from then on that I never ate french fries, didn't like french fries, and, maybe, that I didn't want him to eat them. No. It was a simple piece. For that meal I didn't want french fries. Another friend will, when I tell him I don't know or remember something, argue with me for minutes that yes I do know or remember.

So again when you are listening, try to clearly understand what that person is saying. Could you repeat it? Or at least rephrase it? Is there something you don't understand? Is there something surprising or new? Are you willing to believe that what they say is true for them? When it's your turn, repeat it back a bit if you can and then add whatever you have to add, but it is only then you get to figure out how to say it.

You've seen the poster? The secret to conversation. Take turns speaking. ✿

7 - Love Your Body

Many of these "little things" are about you. You can't change the world unless you are willing to engage with yourself as well as whatever is around you. So hug yourself! Yes, really. Put your left hand on your right shoulder. Put your right hand on your left shoulder. Push hands towards each other. And there you have it. Did it feel a tad strange? Or good? Or interesting?

Are you breathing? (Yes, this is a silly question, although sometimes we hold our breath when we do something different.) But is breathing something you have to think about? Heart pumping? Can you see to read this or can you hear it because someone is reading to you? Can you move? At all? Your body supports you. It just does.

As we look at making a difference, one of the most interesting challenges is to love our own body. This is not something we learn. Society seems to present "them" (bodies) as something that will break down, get sick, age, and be used as a rack for ornamentation. Or otherwise betray us as our true self, that is our mind and soul, gets on with the business of life. St. Francis of Assisi referred to the body as "Brother Ass" reflecting the 13th century asceticism, which is still claimed, that bodies are an uncomfortable accompaniment to being more spiritual.

"Take care of your body" is a conversation for

another day. And an important one. But today, the challenge is to rejoice in being a body. As Frederick Buechner,* in *Wishful Thinking*, says regarding man "it's not that he has a body, but that he is a body." Loving and appreciating our bodies (this isn't always the same thing) is crucial for how we show up in the world and how the world interacts with us. Increasingly this is affirmed by writers and speakers who show us ways to be healthier, happier, and more productive. Do you want or do you seek any of these things? Isn't that one of the reasons you're reading this book? To be healthier, happier, and more productive?

So try it again. Left hand on your right shoulder, right hand on your left, and hug. It is almost that easy. Love your body as it is right now. Whatever the weight. In pain or not. However old you are. As we work toward the gift of being present and so conscious of and participating in the world as it is, our relationship to our bodies becomes central. This is not something we are taught. It is something we need to learn.

If no one is watching you might want to kiss the backs of both of your hands too, to visually offer love and appreciation.

Perhaps it is harder for women with their forced body images? Perhaps it is harder for us all as we are told that we will inevitably slow down and become less attractive as we get older. But seriously loving your body, exactly as it is, provides the base for everything else we have been talking about for changing the world. Loving what is, not putting it down, allows for change. Think about a child. One who is truly loved has permission to flourish rather than struggle to maintain a safe and predictable world. While some, without that permission, also flourish, that isn't the norm. To truly love something is not a stagnant place, but a place of growth. The result of loving yourself, your body, is that you can continue to grow into your ideal self — by your standards — not the mental picture that's been imposed on you by a greedy and unhappy world.

    Amy Ahlers,* in her book *Big Fat Lies Women Tell Themselves*, gives this exercise/challenge: "Stand naked in front of the mirror and name ten things you love about yourself every day for a week. . . .They can range from 'great ass' to 'the miracle of my skin' to 'my heart is pumping.'" I failed this one. I tried, but I literally found myself running from the mirror. What was that response about? Even trying, even that day I ran, began the process. Try that exercise with naming one thing, work up to five, (if you get to ten, let me know. I still need the inspiration). Skin color? Do your nails look good? Wow, can you actually see or feel your hip bones? I never noticed the curve of my neck; my ankles; that one mole that is perfectly placed to be interesting; that my eye color is more varied than I remembered; and I forgot about my dimples. Your turn. Go. Stick with it.

Recently I gained a lot of weight after an illness plus had a lot of leg pain and was suddenly, for the first time in years, really not happy with my body. I felt a bit helpless to do anything about it. Here I was writing all this "love your body" stuff. Hypocrite! But as I fumed and felt guilty I realized I still knew some basics and that my body was still here for me, if I let it. So I've been stretching every morning which helps the pain. By paying attention have lost a little of the weight.

I remembered one more thing: my body is a compass for knowing next steps, what is absolutely the right choice or action. There are two ways to do this, which I'm paraphrasing, adapting, from Martha Beck*. First, learn which direction your body leans when it's attracted to something. Stand up, feet together. Think of something totally icky. Do you lean towards it or away? Now think of something lovely. While most people will lean towards the good and away from the bad, not all will. You just need to know which direction works for you. Another "trick" is to see how your body feels when faced with an opportunity or decision. Are you feeling shut down? Excited, even if a little fearful? Determined, but kinda blah (isn't that a technical term)? Pay attention and you will learn the freedom of how the right direction feels. Practice on little things. I've picked out a shower curtain and declined invitations. Although it is another thing to learn to say yes to what your body says is right and no to the rest when your social expectations and experience say otherwise. Practice.

Somewhere along the way, not by magic, not immediately — unless of course it is immediate — you will start seeing some changes. Maybe not on the scale. Perhaps the pain is still there. But you'll walk a little taller. You'll get more compliments. The weight and the pain will no longer be in charge and there's a great chance the weight will trend towards "ideal" and the pain will become very manageable. You'll be ready for your part in changing the world. So allow me to introduce you to yourself: you in your body — your best self.

Report in. What do you need to do for you? Hug. ✲

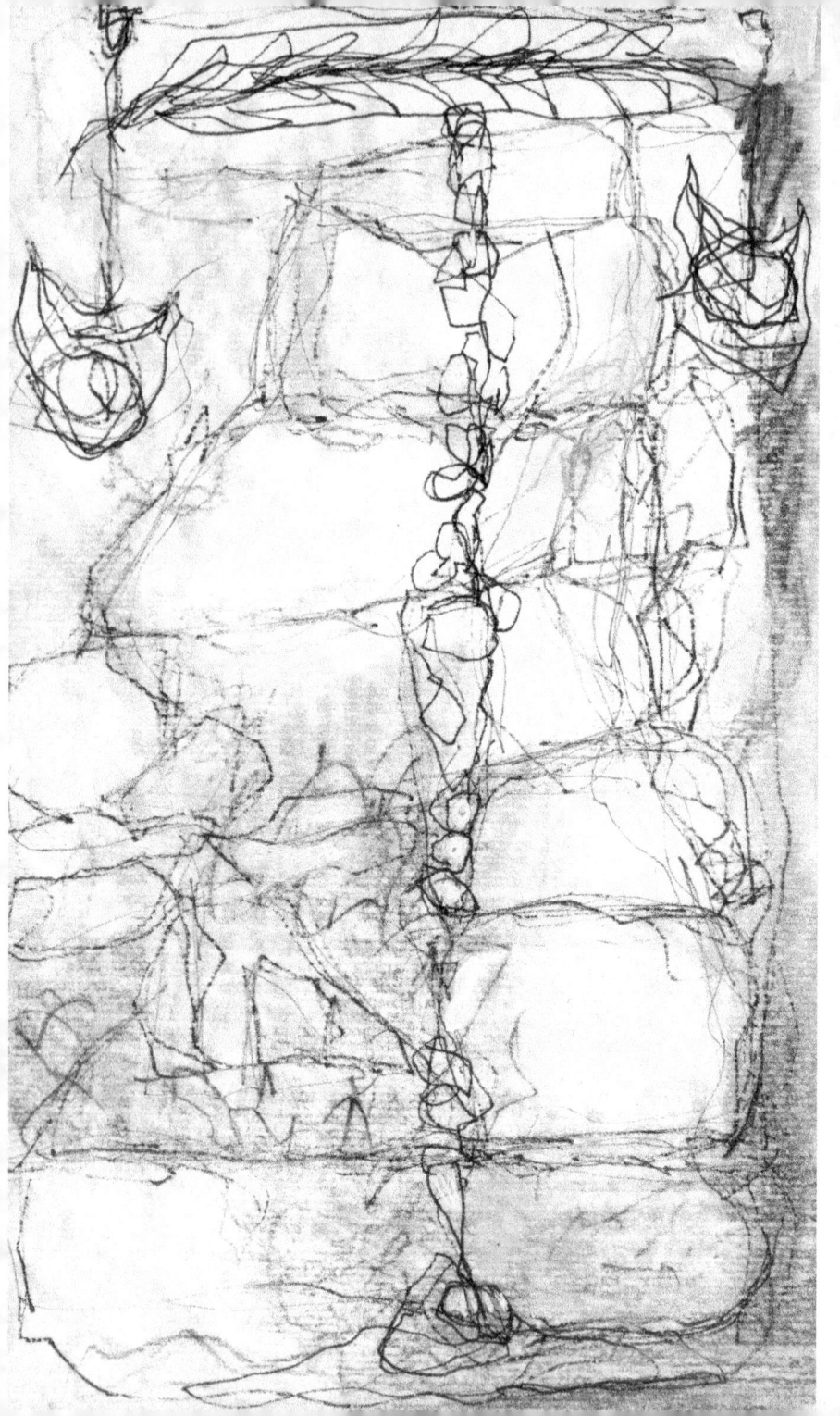

8 - Keep Your Word

Now that we're listening and loving our bodies, we come to one of the most basic interactions we have with others and yourself.

A few years ago, I attended a great conference in Oregon. I'd attended this event the year before and as I traveled to this version I was very excited.

One of the reasons was that a "Let's Change the World!" Spirit Moxie "meetup" had been approved by the event coordinators. The year before I had attended a meetup the afternoon of registration and I'd thought it an exciting beginning to the weekend. So I found a bar/restaurant rumored to have a great, but poorly attended, happy hour and confirmed that they would be happy to have us. Pre-registration was required and the event was "sold out." Almost 40 people said they were coming and there was interest in my Facebook invitation as well.

Eight people showed up, nine if you include me. As far as I could tell none of them had signed up for the event, but came anyway hoping there would be room. The timing was difficult. The announcement said we started at 3 P.M. and registration for the whole event started at 2 P.M. The restaurant had a reputation for being hard to find although I said an orange door was a clue. In the best tradition of events, those who showed up may indeed have been the right people to be there. In any case the conversation was wonderful and rich, and the people there were looking to give and share ideas and inspiration (e.g., how you might recycle those little soaps from hotels on a huge scale).

Although I felt sorry for the bar's owner, and, to be honest, for myself, I shrugged it off until I heard other stories of other meetups where the same thing had happened. As the week went on, the rule seemed to be "even if you didn't sign up, stop by to see if you can get in." I went to one that I'd signed up for and stayed for about ten minutes (hey, I was there). I "really" attended another one that I had signed up for, and I, too, stopped by another meetup that I hadn't signed up for that was full and was told to stay.

I found myself wondering throughout all this about the whole concept of giving your word and keeping it. The RSVP. The shake of the hand. The casual, "I'll call you next week." Any event/party host will tell you that planning has become difficult because people do not let you know if they will attend — or they don't let you know that they won't be there if their plans change. Lawyers have made whole careers around people no longer honoring the handshake and their word. Friendships have been stretched and lovers separated. And I'm certainly not perfect, particularly in the "casual remarks to friends" category.

It has been said that all we have is our word.

As I left the event I was haunted by these two questions: "What is there about keeping your word?" and "Does keeping your word really matter?"

Play with me here. Isn't your world a little easier when someone says they will do something and they actually do it? Pick you up at the airport. Mail that letter. Remember the milk. Repay the money.

And while I think I'm good at this "keep your word" bit, just yesterday I didn't call someone when I said I would. It was on my calendar. I noticed the appointment that morning. But when I saw it, it was after the time and I couldn't get the call to go through.

There are the basic "business" pieces of word keeping too. You were promised a reminder email for the event and it comes. You return the library book. (I get email reminders for that too!) The bus is on time. The airplane makes up the lost time in the air. (Although I'm told by my pilot friends this really isn't possible. So at least the airline knows how to post a schedule that is fairly consistent.) Your reservation is in the system when you get to the hotel. Board members actually come to meetings. The Friday sale begins. The delivery person shows up. And so forth. When these things don't happen we complain on Facebook and to our friends. When they do happen, do we share that the world actually worked?

Another piece is that when we promise something and don't keep that word, it is also a betrayal to ourselves. And when we tell lies, which can be as simple as saying, "I'm fine" when we're not to as obvious as denying we did something we did do, we aren't just lying to the person we're talking to. These are also lies to our bodies. People such as author Martha Beck*, who explore the relationship between lies and our bodies, have observed our bodies, as well as our minds, will remember lies. Lying can actually affect our health. We just talked about loving our bodies. Lying doesn't show love to it at all.

One Sunday I went to an early church service and reported on yet another conference I had attended. "I wish you would come do that at 10:30, too," I was asked, and I responded, "I can do that." I was juggling bus schedules, but easily found a bus (yeah, Google maps) to my favorite breakfast spot. Had a great breakfast, wandered over to the grocery store (did I really need anything?), and thought about going home. No buses for more than 45 minutes. No bus back to church either (had I really promised to do that today or some other Sunday?) But it was only a little over a mile away and the timing would be perfect if I walked. I would arrive about when they needed me to do my spiel, even if it was 90 degrees Fahrenheit out. As I approached the church, I saw a bus pull up that would take me directly home. All

I'd have to do is run or wave or . . . But I walked, watched the bus turn the corner, and went inside the church grateful for air conditioning. When I made sure they knew I was there, the leader said, "Oh, I knew you would be here. You said you would be."

So I did my spiel. Looked at the bus schedule. And found another bus leaving in five minutes for home.

What I have is my word to give, to share. It's free. And your word is yours and actually an integral part of you. How do you honor it? I'm pretty sure the universe will help you keep it. ☼

9 - Vote

9 - Voting

Voting is important, and the most concrete Moxie Move in this book.

At times throughout history casting lots, drawing a name out of a bag, or following some leader's decree has decided things. There are times when a clear consensus determines who should do what. But in today's world, an election results in the most honest reflection of what we think is best for our country or our world. If you have the privilege of voting, you should do that. It's part of freedom, responsibility, and citizenship.

So are you voting? Here in the United States, a disproportionate number of people seem convinced that elections somehow aren't about them. I hear people saying that their vote won't make a difference. That they don't like any of the candidates. That no one who is any good runs for elective office. That it is too much of a hassle. Then we hear of results that aren't popular because people didn't vote.

Through working for women's organizations, I have heard the stories of women's suffrage repeated over and over, so I particularly don't understand women who don't care that in 1917 several women were imprisoned for two months where they were essentially tortured, humiliated, and force fed when they went on a hunger strike so that she, the woman of today who doesn't have time or doesn't really care for the candidates, could go to the polls last year, this year, next year, and every election year in the future and cast a vote.

I don't understand people who don't appreciate the fact that in the United States, we can just walk or drive to the polls and not be hassled at all except by those people standing a prescribed distance from the door campaigning for their candidate. People that don't appreciate that they're not in a country where people risk their lives to go to the polls, where observers from other countries are invited to keep elections honest, and where the voters often don't think much of their choices either, but are grateful that there are choices to be made.

In at least 22 countries voting is mandatory and usually involves a country wide "holiday." There are often consequences. In Australia, for example, you can be fined if you don't vote.

For those into politics, voting is fun. And even the rest of us make a game of it. Spirit Moxie ran a poll on Facebook for the best motto for the Spirit Moxie site, which confirmed "little things that can change the world."

Some games get huge results. For example, during the Christian season of Lent, Forward Movement Publications plays with a certain sports metaphor by creating a "game" called Lent Madness which you can easily find on Facebook or Google. It creates a bracket of saints.

The competition between them is the vote! On each designated day people vote to declare bracket winners, as the competition goes through the days of Lent. Hundreds of people vote daily. The event has almost 5,000 followers on Twitter, more than 20,000 likes on Facebook, and was even mentioned in *Sports Illustrated*! People take sides; even organizations take sides. And it's quite clear that votes count. ("The polls close in an hour and only twenty votes separate the two...") Here politics, voting, a little education, and a sense of play all come together. I've seen people campaign for their favorite saints and I'm told there are parties on election days.

On the national election front in the United States, however, voting somehow can get careless. As we watch the results of elections, it becomes increasingly clear that low voter turn out (because it doesn't matter) has resulted in local and national complications that those not voting (and, of course, some that did vote) find increasingly distressing.

It doesn't have to be difficult or a chore. It shouldn't be. Last year I remember physically wending my way to the office of the Board of Elections because I had just moved and wasn't sure what to do. This year I congratulated a friend who made sure to vote before she headed off on a cruise. Since I don't always know multiple local candidates, I often call someone who does, who also shares my political views, before an election for some input.

While we are considering voting, and changing the world, have you voted for yourself lately? Number 203 in Mike George's* *1,001 Ways to Relax* is "Vote for Yourself." Every morning. He talks about the party of Everliving Happiness, but here we can be leaders in the Make a Difference party. Vote to claim one's own power in changing the world! Today.

So are you willing to vote for fun? Are you willing to vote to affirm yourself? Are you willing to vote because, whatever the issues are where you live, controversial or not, voting says you are willing to help change the world? ✿

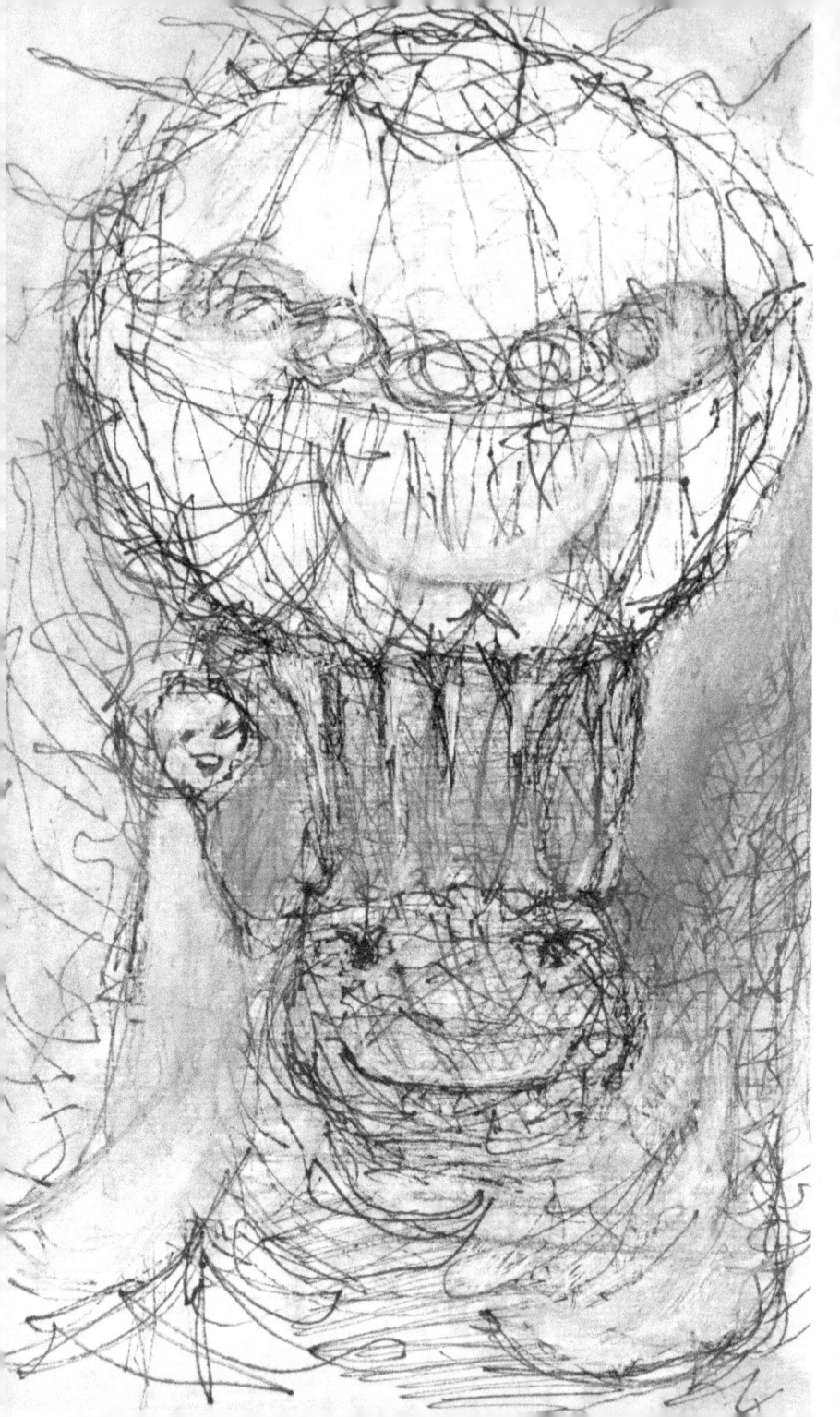

10 - Play

10 - Play

Our last little way to matter, the last little thing to change the world aka the Moxie Moves that we're considering here, is perhaps the most counterintuitive and so, perhaps, the most important. Remember to play.

Some of you do better at this than others. I'm particularly terrible at playing in a conventional sense. (I don't really like games, except for solitaire puzzles, and run from participating in sports - metaphorically, and physically.) It is in play that we reward ourselves, relax, and form friendships outside of work and family. If you play basketball, all that matters is that John has a great hook shot or that Mary has a fast dribble down the court. You don't really need to know he works for your competitor or that she hates everything else you love. Friends who are musicians seem to have this same relationship with each other when practicing and performing. It is when they are playing -- and playing with the music -- that the music seems most alive and engaging.

I do play some Facebook games and most of the people I'm closest with who play these with me, who will do anything for me online, worry about my health, and cheer me on -- heck, I've even parked my car during a conference at one of their houses -- are pretty much my opposite on all the political and social issues. And I'm proud of this. There is something, for me, affirming in having friends of all stripes, so to speak.

Other friends who engage, that is "play," with me do so in the world of food and wine. These friends might agree with me politically and socially, but we don't talk about that. Food and wine are the parameters for our gathering and anything else is just, well, anything else.

I still remember living in a small town where my grand accomplishment was keeping score at softball games, which made me a part of the team. That and recycling beer cans.

Besides personal interaction, it is through a sense of play that our brain is refreshed, becomes open to new possibilities, and so sees things as new and dares to be different. In fact there are effective and pricey play retreats for executives and others to help solve problems and develop new ideas and procedures. They have a great track record when people participate fully without worrying about the results.

Isn't brainstorming a form of play, especially when you don't limit it to practical, possible suggestions? A small non-profit I was connected to suddenly found themselves on an "impossible" river cruise and with a new fund raising option for their 100th anniversary through this kind of brainstorming. As I mention in the opening letter, Spirit Moxie was named through brainstorming.

Dance is a form of play. Learning "real" steps and

dances such as ballroom dancing (on the list of things I'd love to learn) has been proven to alleviate and help prevent dementia. Perhaps this is part of the basic, ideally constant rewiring of the brain.

When we talk about time, play is one way we experience its elasticity. While often a sport is timed, there are multiple examples of time slowing down while someone good in that sport watched a ball move slowly, a defense pattern unfold, time itself stretching into the time needed. It is through a sense of play that the energy needed to do the seemingly impossible becomes almost easy. Play changes the way our brains approach things, which is why work we love is not only easier, but more effective.

Traditionally, and left on their own, children will wrestle with each other, chase each other in a game of tag, play with swords and guns (using sticks if the plastic versions aren't available), shoot the bad guys in video games, and engage in full contact sports like football and rugby. There's health in this. At its best there are rules that add challenges, as well as conversations with parents and other adults. Plus studies show that physical play and creative arts improve how children do in school.

I remember a conversation with my video game obsessed younger son. "You do know this isn't real?"

"Mom [in a 'really do you need to ask' voice],

look." And he held out his scarred palm where his hand had gone through a window. "I know real from virtual. I'm fine."

So play is a way to make distinctions in the world. A way to learn impulses and release feelings of anger and aggression, and, apparently, a way to be healthier and more creative.

In addition there is literally "play acting" such as in role playing games and participating in theatre productions and also in watching plays. Is it play to go to the movies?

Are you dancing?

Have fun. Make a difference in your world, our world. ✿

And Now?

So you've read through all ten of our "little things that can change the world" prompts. Did you learn anything? What Moxie Moves have you done? Did what you do seem to change anything? Most importantly did these actions change you? Note that while some results will be obvious, others won't be immediately visible. So claiming your actions, whether you see results or not, is central. Plus, remember these moves are easy. Have you considered the art and ask what it is saying to you?

If you'd like some guidance, I suggest you take each Moxie Move, in order if you like (yes, even "vote"), and play with it for a week. Do a different variation each day. There are ten suggestions for each topic listed in the following section, although some actions reflect other Moxie Moves as well. For it is only as you change, and know that you matter, yes, you, that the world will also see that it can change—and yes, does change.

Like any good author, this book is certainly written for me. So I'll smile at that person who greeted me like a long lost friend that I don't remember ever having seen before. Give thanks for the gift of present shopping. Take my recycle out to the bin to help clean up my room.

Promise myself a nap. Try a new coffee blend. Listen to one friend's angst about her sister-in-law. Marvel that my pants are loose. Show up at another friend's shop before it closes. Find the Facebook post I promised I'd look at. Vote in Lent Madness because, well, that's play.

You? What does your day look like? Yes, it matters!

Exercises & Suggestions

Today do at least one of the challenges listed below:

Smile

- Smile, and in your heart wish well, all the people who serve you, such as those working in grocery stores or restaurants.
- Smile at yourself in the mirror and say, silently or aloud, "I love you." Do this at least three different times.
- Look at strangers as you go about your day and smile at at least five of them. Extra points if they engage and smile back, but, if they don't, smile anyway!
- Greet your friends and family with a smile.
- If you're working through something difficult, look up and smile at the person working with you or smile at yourself. How is that smile different?
- Smile at all the animals you meet. Dogs. Birds. Can you include spiders, ants, and bees?
- Smile while you're working out, walking, or doing something like yoga. Or just walking upstairs or across the room.
- Smile at small children. Notice their reactions.
- How do you smile in pictures? Do you like that smile? Practice different smiles with selfies or a friend willing to take multiple shots.
- Smile, often. Even if no one else is around.

Be Grateful

- Say thank you before eating. Anything. It doesn't have to be aloud. If you are not into verbally praying in some form when with others, raising a toast works as a way to share your thanks.
- Before you get up in the morning, remember five specific things you're grateful for that happened the day before.
- Look up. What are three things you see that you are thankful for/can delight in, the more specific the better.
- Set a timer for 10 minutes and write (yes on paper, not in your head) about the best of the last three months.
- What are your favorite colors? Where do you see them right now?
- What new thing have you learned about yourself this week?
- Whom have you met for the first time this week? (Yes, the new checkout girl at the grocery store counts. But maybe you should get out a bit more?)
- What TV shows do you really enjoy? Watch one.
- Hold a baby. Or pet a puppy or kitten. Yes. That feeling is gratitude too.
- Drink a glass of water. Slowly. Enjoy!

Sleep

- Go to bed. Get up 6-9 hours later.
- Take a nap.
- Notice when you feel tired. Do you want sleep? Have you just eaten? Had a drink? Is whatever you're doing incredibly dull? Just notice.
- If you have a device that can monitor your sleep (a Fitbit or an Apple Watch for example) wear it for a least two nights. (Yes, there are free apps for an Apple Watch that can do this.)
- Do certain sounds make you sleep better? Or does quiet seem essential? Experiment.
- How do you react to light when you sleep? Does complete darkness, including no lights from electronics, help? Maybe you can try a sleep mask. Notice.
- Go to bed. Get up 6-9 hours later. Repeat.
- This week, track how you feel when you wake up (raring to go? still tired?) How much sleep did you get and how sound was it. Did you dream?
- Take a nap.
- Go to bed.

Be Litter Free

- Be conscious of throwing all bits of trash away.
- Clean up a corner of your bedroom. This could be cleaning a drawer – or folding and putting away clothes. Neat and organized looks different to everyone.
- Remind someone to pick up something they dropped.
- Notice where the trash cans/bins are. If you were designing a street or a room, where would you put them?
- Pick up and throw away something you notice someone else has left around. A foam cup on a bench, a gum wrapper, anything.
- Consider the image of litter as "weeds." Right around where you are sitting, what needs moving whether into a trash can or into a drawer? Do it.
- Empty the trash cans into the garbage can for pick up. An overflowing trash can is litter too.
- Get rid of some of the duplicate, unneeded files on your computer. Delete the duplicate, blurry pictures. These also litter your life. What about the people in your address book that you don't even remember? Remove at least 20 files, pictures, or unneeded addresses.
- Learn more about the effect of litter on wildlife. Share.
- How are you "littering" your mind and body. Write or draw about it.

Learn

- Well? Try it. I never knew I could get two kinds of iced mocha at my coffee place until the day I wrote this. Yes, it can be that easy.
- Find a new route home. It doesn't matter if it's shorter or longer or more boring or more interesting or....
- What interests a friend that you never thought about? Explore those interests. My friends right now are into Goth music and making mead.
- Relearn something you've forgotten or become "rusty" in. French? A martial arts form? A craft?
- How do you use that thing over there? (Or in a catalog or on TV.)
- What is the name of that plant/style of architecture/poetry style — whatever catches your eye?
- Learn a new game.
- What is your major hobby or passion? Find something new about that... "There's always something."
- Practice writing, drawing, or even playing a game with your non-dominant hand.
- Figure out a new activity for this challenge or one of the previous or subsequent challenges. Do it. Share it!

Listen

- Shut your eyes for a minute (as soon as it's safe). What do you hear?
- Repeat back to someone what you just heard them say. ("So you're saying.....")
- Try to identify songs and artists. Check to see how you're doing.
- What is the smallest, most distant, sound you can hear?
- Be around someone who, by your standards, doesn't speak clearly (tone, accent, phrasing) and try to "get it" the first time they share. If you don't, ask them to repeat until you do. (Yes, that many times...)
- Notice the range of pitch and volume you can hear. Really concentrate.
- Use earplugs, especially somewhere with loud sound volume.
- Take turns speaking. Try not deciding what you want to say while the other person is talking. (Yes, I know this is hard.)
- Find a form of music with which you aren't terribly familiar. Listen carefully. Do you like it? Why do you think others like it?
- Just listen to that speech or presentation. Practice trying to not judge or respond.

Exercises & Suggestions Moxie Moves

Love Your Body

- Give yourself a hug.
- Look at your body (preferably naked) in the mirror and name five things, however small, you appreciate. Do this for four days.
- Exercise in some different way. Or at least find a new place to walk.
- Get a massage.
- Sleep (see above).
- Learn what colors and styles look great on you. Wear them.
- Comb your hair.
- Take a bath. Add Epsom salts or bubbles.
- Stretch.
- Kiss the backs of your hands a couple times a day. Yes, you're that amazing.

Keep Your Word

- Make a list of all the promises you make today.
- Return your library books on time. (You do use the library, right? If not, check it out.)
- What are the expectations in one of your current relationships? Talk with that person about them to see how you're doing.
- Show up as promised.
- Did you say you'd do something such as like a Facebook post, call a friend, or put the dishes away? Do it.
- What are your dreams? Do one step towards them as a promise to yourself.
- RSVP - and honor it. If you have to change your plans (but try not to), make sure you let your host know.
- What does it mean, to you, to make your word your priority? Write a little about this.
- Do you dare use a handshake as a binding promise? Try it on something little and make sure you follow through.
- Do a text or email version of the handshake promise. Make a plan or promise. Follow through.

Vote

- Are you registered to vote? If not, register. If so, check that you have what you need to vote and where your polling place is located.
- Vote in something. A photography contest. An online competition. There's always something....
- Start following the candidates for the next election in your area. Trust me. No matter when you're reading this, someone is running for office.
- Voice your opinion on something, preferably directly to another person - friend or politician.
- Answer some poll or survey as to preferences. Food choices, colors, activities? This is good practice for learning to express your opinion.
- Listen (see above) to someone you don't agree with. Don't argue, just see if you can understand their point of view.
- Create your own poll, perhaps as a game, and notice your response to the results.
- Put voting dates (including those for primaries) on your calendar.
- Run for an office — can be for an organization if you like. Or campaign for someone who is running.
- Every morning when you get up, mentally vote for yourself as "most likely to change the world."

Play

- Use your non-dominant hand for whatever - to write for a bit, eat a meal, tap on your phone...
- Learn a new game.
- Watch some sort of play (a performance, a ball game, kids in the yard) with someone else. What do you notice?
- Spend time with a dog throwing a stick or ball. Or with a cat with a piece of string or a laser pointer.
- Borrow a young child (or spend special time with yours) and just do what they want to. Sit on the floor and just explore, be silly, sing.... Report in!
- Go for a walk by yourself with no destination or agenda. Go where your body leads.
- Throw a party, or go to one.
- Dance. Dancing around the living room counts.
- Sing in the shower. Hey, it's a known art form!
- Play with words and ideas either in writing or with a friend.

Appendix

Congratulations. You've now explored and, I trust, practiced ten different ways to change the world and yourself. Or maybe change yourself and with it the world. You've looked at the art to get a different perspective on each "little thing" and perhaps imagined how you interpret those words.

      Because if we do these Moxie Moves and their related actions, a critical mass will be created that can result in exciting, if unexpected, positive change. Simply because this is how energy works. Meanwhile, if you want more, make certain, if you're on Facebook, you've liked the Spirit Moxie page plus make sure you're signed up on *www.spiritmoxie.com* for the very occasional email updates that explore more of these little things.

For some ongoing challenges simply do these:

- Hold the door open for someone. Say "thank you" if they hold it for you.
- Use available revolving doors, if you can.
- Breathe. Be still. Take a deep breath in. Feel it in your body. Let it all out.

- Learn to say "thank you" in at least three other languages. Practice.
- Give someone a present, and/or make a donation.
- Explore a new technology. No excuses.
- Learn an "old" way to do something. Develop a photo. Poach an egg. Draft a letter, a blueprint, or some music. (I'd love to hear what you try.)
- Take public transportation somewhere. Yes, an airplane counts, but extra points for a bus, streetcar, or local train.
- Check out the *Resources listed at the end of this book.
- Walk in the rain, or dance in it.
- Hold a baby, a baby animal counts.
- Write or draw your response to each of the Moxie Moves.
- Add to this list
- Claim that what you do matters.

*Resources

All effects and implications indicated in *Moxie Moves*, such how not littering might affect crime levels and property values, can be verified by a simple online search. Multiple sources were consulted for this information, but they are not referenced within the text.

Shawn Achor, *The Happiness Advantage: the seven principles of positive psychology that fuel success and performance at work* (New York: Broadway Books, 2010)

Amy Ahlers, *Big Fat Lies Women Tell Themselves: ditch your inner critic and wake up you inner superstar* (Navato, CA: New World Library, 2011)

Martha Nibley Beck, *Finding Your Way in a Wild New World: reclaim your true nature to create the life you want* (New York: Free Press, 2011)

Frederick Buechner, *Wishful Thinking: a theological abc* (San Francisco: Harper & Row, 1990)

Lewis Carroll, *Alice's Adventures in Wonderland* (London: Macmillan, 1865)

Mike Dooley, *www.tut.com*, hand kissing exercise

Mike George, *1,001 Ways to Relax* (San Francisco: Chronicle Books, 2003)

Robin Hobbs, *Royal Assassin: the farseer trilogy book II* (New York: Random House, 1996)

J. A. Jance, *The A List* (New York: Gallery Books, 2019)

Andrew Newberg and Mark Robert Walkman, *How God Changes Your Brain: breakthrough findings from a leading neuroscientist* (New York: Random House, 2009)

Lissa Rankin, MD, *The Anatomy of a Calling: a doctor's journey from the head to the heart and a prescription for finding your life's purpose* (New York: Rodale, 2015)

SARK-author/artist, self hug exercise

Eckhart Tolle, *The Power of Now: a guide to spiritual enlightenment* (Navato, CA: New World Library, 1997)

The Artist

Cynthia (Cynthia Jane Collins, M.Div., M.S., L.M.F.T.) is a feminist hippie from the 1960s, an artist, and a teacher on a rich journey. Her practices span the decades and a wide spectrum—from teaching artistic realism, to studio work in non-objective mixed media, to spiritual paintings and art journaling. She invites students or viewers to open doorways to the soul. She personally loves competent rebellion, sheep, chocolate, and gathering art supplies. Quoting her favorite philosophers, her grandchildren, she wishes "happy to you!" and "Yay!!!"

She can be reached at www.cynthiajanecollinsstudios.com

The Art

The art illustrating this book was created by reading the simple word titles for each Moxie Move—not the full text. Cynthia contemplated each of these titles which resulted in nuanced and deepened responses. The artistic interpretation through the images is thus layered and multimedia. The hope is that the visual work will encourage you to discover what the words mean for you.

The Author

Photo by Mark Stucker

B (Sally B. Sedgwick, M.A., M.F.A., D.Min.) has lived in places as varied as New York City and Nenana, Alaska, and through these adventures has developed an ongoing commitment to exploring possibilities and new ideas. In service to this, she created Spirit Moxie and has done things like drying dishes in Paris, walking on fire, and happily spending time in multiple airports. While she shouldn't be allowed to participate in activities involving managing paper or doing handcrafts. she loves to cook, dance, and read mysteries. An introvert who loves parties, B welcomes thoughtful conversations over great food, good coffee, or a long walk.

Visit her at www.spiritmoxie.com

www.ingramcontent.com/pod-product-compliance
Lightning Source LLC
Chambersburg PA
CBHW071215070526
44584CB00019B/3035